SONGS WITHOUT SOUND

Lyrical journeys of wonder and words

by Deke

Important

Print ISBN 979-8-9904536-7-8

Rodney Richards, Editor, ABLiA Media LLC
Tumpa01765, Graphic Designer and Illustrator

First edition

AI was not used to create content.

Contents

To

To my loving and supportive wife Kathleen—my quiet strength—thank you for believing in me when I struggled to believe in myself. Your patience, strength, and constant encouragement made this book possible. I am forever grateful to walk this journey by your side.

To my wonderful caring children, Harmony and Cline, the heartbeat behind every verse and the home where my heart always returns. Thank you for your love, your laughter, and the joy you bring to my life every day. You inspire me to be better, to dream bigger, and to keep going. This is for you.

To my many friends, who laughed with and at me, you carried me through the first drafts and encouraged me to keep the ink moving. You are all here with me in one form or another.

Without each of you, these words would be echoes in the dark. Thank you for being the light that shapes every line.

Preface

I don’t write from perfection; I write from the middle of things—from lessons still unfolding and the scars that still speak, as well as the joys of life.

If these words reach you, it's because we share the human thread of wanting to rise again, no matter how heavy the fall. Every songwriter knows that silence can sing louder than a chord. In these *Songs without Sound*, the music drifts inward.

It seeps into thought, reflection, and quiet places where emotions echo long after the last note fades. These poems are verses unscored, melodies written in ink instead of air. Each line hums with rhythm, memory, and the subtle aches of what’s left unsaid.

From moments of stillness to waves of longing, *Songs without Sound* is a collection for those who hear music in their solitude and find harmony in the spaces between words and feelings.

Part One: Wounds and Wings

These poems trace the journey from
ache to ascent—where wounds
become wings and
sorrow softens
into peace.

Each carries loss toward light,
reminding us that wounds do not end us,
they teach us to fly.

Words of Love

In realms of speech, where words take flight
let kindness be our guiding light
for words of love, a gentle stream
can heal a heart, fulfill a dream

Words of hate, a bitter sting
leaves scars behind, on everything
they build up walls, and tear apart
the fragile bonds within the heart

So let us choose with mindful care
the words we speak, the thoughts we share
let love's sweet song forever play
and chase all hate-filled words away

Words of love, not words of hate
let this be our chosen fate
to build a world, where all can see
the power of love within you and me

Morning Prayer

I seek your light, to straighten my wandering way
to find the peace that dawns with every day
Oh, Holy Mother, hear my humble plea
Forgive me Jesus, for thinking only of me

The foolish things I've done, the chances I have missed
the times I hit the ground; when my weaknesses could not resist
Oh, Holy Mother, on my knees I pray
Forgive me Jesus, for letting my demons in to play

I hear your whispers, soft as summer rain
a gentle promise, easing every pain
Your love surrounds me, like the vast blue sky
Forgive me Jesus, for doing just enough to get by

Thank God

Thank God for the rain,
it helps to wash away my pain
Thank God for the winds,
caressing my heart as it mends.
Thank God for nature's sweet song
reminding me, where I belong
Thank God for the light of day
for chasing the shadows away
Thank God for new seeds
nourishing our lives with what we need
Thank God for all of you,
the joy, love, and time we knew

Double Handed

One hand alone
a struggle to impart
A task half-done
a heavy fractured heart.

Limits bind a path
that seems so long
Frustration builds
a silent bitter song.

But with hands entwined
a double-handed clasp;
thumb upon thumb
a spiritual grasp.

A whispered prayer, and
faith takes hold
Burdens lift, and
free my weary soul.

February 19th

The nineteenth of the second month
A time that whispers of beginnings and ends
A date where emotions take a stance
A place where joy and sorrow hold hands and dance

The nineteenth of the second month
Laughter mingles with tears, not fully dried
On this day, in the merger of beginning and decay
two were born and two have passed away

The nineteenth of the second month
is a cradle of memories I'll always hold
Forever to cast its long shadows and radiant lights
on a bittersweet blend of heartfelt grief and loving
delight

Warmth and Light

When the sunlight left your body,
it didn't just fade into the night.
It painted the sky with a story,
of warmth and light's gentle fight.

When the sun kissed your skin goodbye,
it left a warmth that would never die.
The world grew still, and in that tender hush,
the light retreated into a mournful, gentle touch.

The warmth and light, did not abandon you,
it only changed, its loving shade of hue.
From a fiery gold to moonlit white,
guiding you to the blessed eternal night.

Now in every dawn that breaks anew,
and in every sunset's amber view,
your essence lives, forever bright.
A confirmation to your warmth and light.

The Healing

A hollow silence where laughter used to bloom,
now memories reign, a shadow in every room

Mementoes in cartons rising from the floor,
picking up the pieces, seems there's always one more

A haunting task, a lonely exhausting climb,
the healing of a broken heart, one precious fragment at a time

Searching through remnants of yesterday's cheer,
unraveling thoughts, cherishing every tear

The past gently cradled, a part of the whole,
in the garden of healing, God nurtures my soul

My Reunion

The invitation came, a reunion's celestial call,
a gathering of loved ones, beyond the mortal wall.
I see mom, her smile warm and bright,
her heart a beacon in the ethereal night
she's waiting there, with open loving arms
to shelter me from sorrows, shield me from harm

Dad's there too, with his twinkling knowing eyes,
he'll tell me stories of the grand cosmic skies.
His laughter, rich and warm, a comforting embrace
erasing time's wrinkles, etched upon my face.

And Uncle Jay, the joker, always quick to tease
he greets me with a riddle, meant to set me at ease.
I see my friends, who left me behind
band mates, Logie and Minos, forever in my mind.

My loving niece and sister, my older brother too
like fireflies in the night, doing what they do.
I know there will be healing, a mending of the soul,
a letting go of burdens, making my spirit whole.

Forgiveness offered, understanding found
in my reunion, on hallowed, sacred ground

I Remember You

I remember you, in every winter's frost
a pristine icy landscape, mirroring what I lost

I remember you, in the promise of spring
an ache within my heart, like a bullet ant's sting
.
I remember you, on a starry summer night
dancing among the constellations, under heaven's porchlight

I remember you, in the rustling of autumn leaves
a vibrant, fleeting beauty brings me to my knees

I remember you, and in that memory, you live
a piece of you forever, a gift you still give

If I Were

If I were someone else today,
I'd wake without the weight of my shame,
test how it feels to move through rooms
where no one knew my name.

If I were someone braver than me,
I'd speak the truth without disguise,
swallow the things I've said aloud,
and not react when voices rise.

If I were the one I judged the most,
I'd listen longer than I speak,
learn how fear wears many masks
and strength is often quiet, weak.

If I were the person I once loved,
I'd trace the scars I couldn't see,
understand how silence grows
when love is offered sparingly.

If I were the better version of myself,
I'd honor all she gave and shared,
put her heart above my own
and carry every worry she bared.

Silent Burdens

If the cross you drag is self-disdain
a beam carved from memory
Don't think that only lasting pain
is the price you owe constantly.

If you wake before the break of day
with yesterday still in your chest
No dawn can chase thoughts away
that will not let your spirit rest

If you carry crosses branded with blame
for broken promises and words unsaid
Don't craft your heart from your own shame
pray for mercy and leave the past among the dead

If you pray for forgiveness, yet still hide
denying yourself worthy of Our Lord's grace
the weight you bear still multiplies
in shadows you think no light can erase

Listen close, somewhere deep a whisper calls
and your silent burdens will begin to fade
a gentler hand will catch your fall
when a tender peace within is made

Strength

She never knew how strong she was
until silence asked her to decide
whether to keep the wound alive
or lay the knife down at her side

She never knew how strong she was
until forgiveness freed her mind
allowing her to drop the shield
and leave the bitterness behind

He never knew how strong he was
when a memory pulled him back inside
tempting him to feed old pain
and let the past remain his guide

He never knew how strong he was
when sorrow knocked upon the door
not hardened by what tried to break him
but made his heart whole once more

I never knew how strong I was
until I had to forgive someone who wasn't sorry
I chose to rise above the pain
and let His Grace rewrite my story

We never know how strong we are
until we trust what we can't see
and find the peace that holds us close
and anchors our heart eternally

A Father's Ramblings

A father rambles,
    in a voice soft and low
landing on tender ears,
    lessons to help them grow

Be kind to all you meet,
    be humble and be grand
for kindness is the beacon,
    that lights the darkest land

When you face your shadows,
    and self-doubt crosses your mind
be true to yourself, have faith in the Lord,
    and your path will realign

The Gardener

He was a gardener, with thumbs of green
a gentle soul he was, one few have ever seen
he sowed his seeds with pure delight
his garden patch, a flourishing sight

But more than plants he fed
with water, sun, and care
his children bloomed instead
like flowers beyond compare

He taught them kindness, truth, and grace
as he tended to each fragile shoot
he watched them grow, in time and space
each bearing lush and loving fruit

His love was fertilizer, oh so true
helping each of their spirit's soar
reaching the skies of endless blue
a gardener's love, asks for nothing more

Fractures

In quiet moments as the world fades to black
a fracture deepens within a splintered crack
There's an upsurge in pain, clickety-clack
inhaling deeply as she fights another setback

She tells herself, life is not about the breaks
but how we choose to mend, as our life shakes
A quiet strength moans, as her faith awakes
a beautiful human blooms, despite deep body aches

Snowflake

A snowflake landing on the tip of her nose,
reflections gently kissing inside windows.
A snowflake landing in her inner ear,
whispering secrets only she can hear.

A snowflake landing on the lash of her eye,
bowing with blinks, delicate and shy.
A snowflake landing in the palm of her hand,
disappointment drifting across the desert sand.

A snowflake spoke with a devilish tongue,
words of deceit, rehearsed, beautifully sung.
A snowflake smothered under the sole of her shoe,
a head held high, walking away from the likes of you.

Dragonflies

Dragonflies shimmer
where day meets night
carrying meanings in wings of light---
whispers of truths the heart can't deny
told in the hush of their passing by

So when one hovers close and sly
a living jewel against the sky---
listen well, for its message is true
the Lord our God, truly loves you

In and Out

It's easy to count what crosses our lips---
measured in calories or the width of our hips.
We measure the salt, sugar, coffee, and bread,
but more important than what we swallow,
are the words and phrases that are sometimes said.

The mouth is a doorway both narrow and wide,
where kindness or cruelty start,
and what passes through is carried along
to live in another's heart.

Speak as if each word has an aftertaste
choose words wisely before they depart.
Long after silence has taken their place,
their flavor remains in the heart.

Speak as if someone you love might be near
hearing each word you say,
for words once spoken belong to the world
and never fade away.

So speak with a heart that leans towards light,
let mercy be a part of your art.
For the richest reward that our life can hold
is the place in a well-spoken heart.

The Silent Reckoning

At dawn he dressed in borrowed sun,
pretending all the fights were won.
Yet in the hush before the day,
he mourned the parts he gave away.

He bent his days to fit their need,
rearranged his life at reckless speed.
He gave both hands when one would do,
ignoring what it cost him too.

The mirror learned to hold its breath,
watching him barter bits of self.
He smiled so no one would see the seams,
or hear the cracking of his dreams.

He swallowed doubt and named it love,
believed the weight was sent from above.
Through storms that tried to pull him down,
he wore resilience like a crown.

He aged in favors left unpaid,
a debt to self he never made.
His heart still lent what it could spare,
and cloaked his sorrow in a prayer.

At last he rests where shadows fade,
a misunderstood soul, a renegade.
His heart now free from every snare,
his mind made whole in answered prayers.

Locked-In

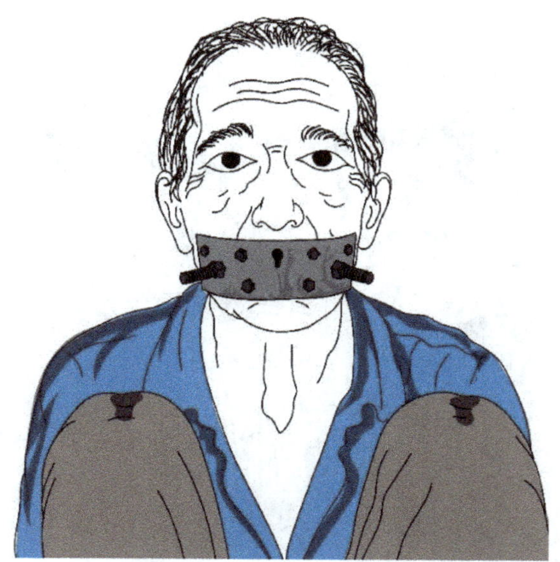

Somewhere in a hollow chest,
between hurting shoulders and aching feet,
there's a dust covered empty nest
lined with past visitor's timesheets.

Somewhere in an overcrowded mind
among the chemicals and memories,
there's a glimmer of someone in decline,
struggling to survive within restricted boundaries.

Somewhere between the scars and wrinkled skin,
stretched tattoos no longer have a beginning or end.

Between the opaque window of my mind,
and my mouth's bolted door, there's an erosion
taking place that can't be ignored.

If I do forget the world, remember this for me,
I knew your love even when I lost me.

Encounter

Would you recognize me if I walked up to you today?
Might you joyfully embrace me?
Or quickly turn your head away?
Will your eyes swell and water the garden within?
Or will your tongue take stage and perform again?

Could you recognize me if I looked different from you?
If I speak an unfamiliar language, what will you do?
If my body is a work of art, will you still see me___
through the piercings and tattoos?
If I offer you a hand, will you ask for two?
Will you only accept it if it is shiny and new?

Will you speak to me if my words touch your ears?
Will you step aside and hang out with the non-
volunteers?
If my words sing out, will you recognize the melody?
Will you happily sing along, or remain deaf for eternity?

The Fading

I witnessed your mind loosen its grip,
thoughts drifting like ash from a distant flame.
I watched your eyes search faces for their name,
each one dissolving as the throat swallows another sip.

Like a needle on vinyl when the record skips,
    you ask the same soft question twice, then twice
    again, it spills from your lips.

Time grows cruel in unsuspecting ways,
it takes life without a sound, leaving only love
    to do the labor throughout the hardest days.

And when at last the fading ends,
and earthly knowing ceases,
the mind will be made whole again
from all its scattered pieces.

What time erased will be returned,
and nothing precious left behind,
each wrinkle, scar, and memory earned
is a testament to a life refined.

You Are Allowed

You are not weak
for wanting peace.
You are not wrong
for wanting release.

No hand has the right
to silence your claim.
No love demands
that you live in pain.

You may walk away.
You may close the door.
Your heart is sacred---
it serves more.

Walk.
Speak.
Breathe.
You are allowed.

Part Two: Memories in Motion

These poems move through time's soft echoes,
where love lingers,
memories stir, and
questions drift,
like leaves on a restless wind.

Each poem is a step through time's tender dance.

Original painting by Hannah Robinson

Moments in Time

It's funny how the artist of the mind,
creates a kaleidoscope of moments in time.
Each shard reflects a past love or friend,
mingled with family as the canvas extends.

It's amazing to me,
how the things we forget are often clear to see.
Some are recalled in moments of déjà vu,
others are hazy, dancing in and out of view.

We all keep painting our own masterpiece,
some may be sudden, while others time-released.

It's funny how the composer of the heart,
creates a song from life topping all charts.
Each note a memory of varied years,
most filled with laughter; others seem to leer.

It's amazing to me,
how life events create a melody.
We all keep crafting our musical score,
each draft a change of genre, from the one before.

Artistry at work,
two lives in rhyme,
each has a special place,
a beloved moment in time.

Today's Rhymes

So, what will these rhymes do today?
Will they draw me close or lead me astray
Will they make me laugh or only take me halfway

So, what will these rhymes do today?
Will they place the truth of a memory on display
Or will they remind me of one who passed away

So, what will these rhymes do today?
Will they take a shot or share a glass of chardonnay
Will they do nothing at all and leave me in silence to
pray

Love Letters in the Sand

No ink, no paper, just a fingertip
carving stories in the sand.
Two Hearts in partnership
within a thought's tender hand

"Dear heart," one wrote, "with you I find,
your touch a breeze that stirs my mind."
The curves of letters which waves will trace,
such quiet devotion, time cannot erase.

The second penned in a reply along the shore,
"Forever with you," she wrote once more.
    "Your touch, a feathered brush sending shivers
    down my spine, in the pulse of the seasons,
    our hearts aligned."

As dawn awakes and paints the morning shore,
your lips on mine, a soft gently placed encore.
The tide may wash away the words we write
but nothing can erase the passion you ignite.

Movie of Love

I'm her leading man in our Movie of Love
our names in lights on the marquee above
It's a passion play, starring she and I
she plays the ladybug, I the dragonfly

She's my leading lady in our movie of love
we fit the parts so well, like a custom-made glove
The only script is what's written in our hearts
we knew each other's lines from the very start

There're no extras written into our script
no understudy could ever be equipped
No need for stunt men when the curtains are closed
the bestselling soundtrack ever composed

Not looking for Oscars, just a love that's true
take after take we've seen this through
Red carpet scenes shot by candlelight
where each frame unfolds beneath the fall of night

Between the Grooves

Beneath the needle's tender touch,
a surge of memories I love so much.
Between the grooves a diamond finds its way,
merging melodies with visions of yesterday and today.

Each note a pulse of my heart's refrain,
what passions lay dormant, in golden light
and silver rain.
Between the grooves, I linger and drift,
o recalling each treasured song, oh what a gift!

To dive into sound where memories collide,
where the past and present sit side by side.
Between the grooves, oh how my heart is full,
to the artist I bow, and to share them with you,
I'm extremely grateful.

Twilight In Bloom

In the hush of Spring's dimming veil and grace
two hearts entwine in their secret place.
Where whispers are soft as sweet perfume
few things are warmer than our shared room

Fingers lightly dance with a tender glide
with eyes tightly closed, I see you by my side.
With every sigh, the world blurs, fades away
lost in April's twilight where shadows come to play

She Knew

She knew the depths, the shallow side,
the parts that hid when darkness cried.
A heart that beats with love so true,
for her alone, this she knew.

She knew the stranger, an enigma's flaw,
a quiver in the shadows, unfiltered and raw.
Contradictions, stark, bold and few,
secrets unshared, this she knew.

She knew his failings, the guilt he bore,
and loved him still, more than before.
She saw the selfish side, a fleeting view,
his giving nature, this too, she knew.

She knew him, the one so hard to tame,
a spirit wild, a flickering flame.
Yet in the depths, she found true value,
a man worth keeping, this she knew.

The Ballad of K & D

In the heart of Louisiana's deep,
where cypress trees stand tall and willows weep,
there lived a man with an aura intense and free,
a Cajun's heart, mimicking an oak tree's canopy.

Far away in the pulse of a city's bustling maze,
a lady lived, her world busy and multi-phased.
A New Yorker, with a mind sharp and keen,
yearning for something more than what is seen.

One fateful day their paths did intertwine,
but it was unlike either to date online.
He found himself enchanted in her fairy's spell,
she equally intrigued, her thoughts on his carousel.

He spoke of swamps and marshes, of an alligator's might,
she told of skyscrapers, and the city's never dimming lights,
They shared their worlds, so different yet so grand,
a gumbo of cultures, a path they could not withstand.

Though their backgrounds differed, there was common
ground, in the depths of the future, true love abounds.
Between the bold Cajun man, and the city lady fair,
a love transcending, both fully aware.

Encourage Me

Are you sure you want to encourage me?
You'll only provoke my curiosity.
For once the seed of thought is sown,
a wild adventure will soon be shown.

You see; my mind is a restless sea,
a place where dreams roam wild and spirits free.
Encouragement is the spark, igniting an exotic flame,
a thrill is born, excitement with no shame.

If you dare, hold onto my hand tight,
we'll chase the shadows, embrace the night.
Remember well, oh friend, so bold,
in curiosity, the undaunted beholds.

Yet should you retreat, think twice my dear,
for withdrawal pulls the daring near.
But if you want to live audaciously,
by all means, go ahead—encourage me.

FAIS
DO-DO

Ah-ka-dee

Before the sun rises over moss-draped trees,
the smell of Community coffee floats on the breeze
Bayou mornings glow, sticky and sweet
LeJeune's French bread and boudin, bon appétit

Oncle Perry grabs his hat, fishing pole in hand
tells of a monster catfish on Thibodeaux's land
Tante Mae rolls her eyes while stirring the roux
Flavors rich, and always bon goût

Before noon the music's playing, just like that, voilà
Neighbors gatherer, "Bonjour! Comment ça va?"
Cajun hearts stay warm beneath southern skies,
Louisiana festivals live and laughter never dies.

Hands held in friendship, voices join à nous
To a stranger they may think we're all trop fou.
Life flows sweet, when bayous, moss, and music combine,
every Cajun knows it fais-do-do time

May every bayou bend and moss-draped tree
keep watch over the souls who dance and dream free
May our Cajun songs carry peace in its rhyme,
and may Ah-ka-dee bless your soul for all time.

Mind or Brain?

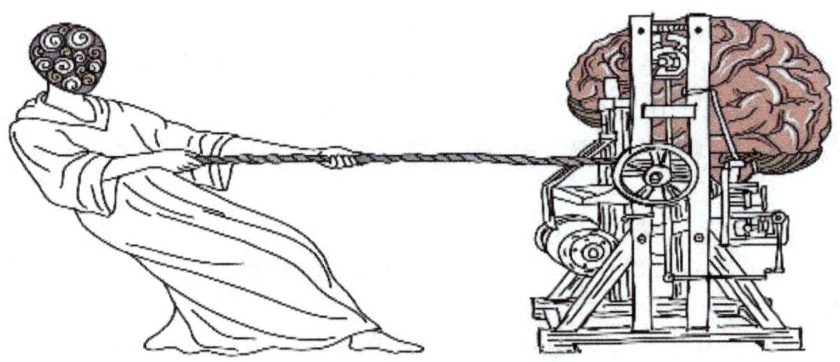

A whisper in the skull provokes a furrowed brow.
Mind or brain, which dictates now?
The sudden catch of a breath held tight,
a surge of thoughts, in and out of sight.

Her mind is a network, intricate and fine,
a firing synapses of a complex design.
Her brain is circuitry, robust and vast,
of neural pathways holding fast.

Her mind is a weaver, crafting dreams,
interpreting life in swirling streams.
Her brain is the loom, efficient and strong,
but the patterns woven, where do they belong?

The answers lay beyond the reach
of scientific fact or reasoned speech.
A mystery held within her soul,
beyond her brain's or mind's control.

Room without a View

Between the seen and unseen
where shadows play peekaboo with the light
there's complete absence, no one in sight

Among the heard and unheard
where whispers blend secrets into emptiness
vanishing vowels and swallowed syllables
are part of the process

For in the room without a view
Where no one peers to judge what's true
when only a single shadow is cast
a heart can then speak its truth at last

Think Twice

If you think you've heard what I said,
think twice, it was only a spark
ricocheting in my head.

If you think you know who I am,
think twice, you've missed the real man.
You've shaken hands with what I show
not what I carry, not what I know.

If you think my silence is peace
think twice, it's a war on a leash
Some battles never make a sound
they're fought where no one gathers around.

If you think my kindness is weak
think twice, it's strength I wish to speak.
It takes more power to stand still
than strike back hard with sharpened will.

If you think my scars are shame
think twice, you've forgotten my name.
Every crack you think you see
is proof of what did not break me.

If you think I'm easy to read
think twice, I am more than you see.
The surface rarely says it right,
there's depth beneath what meets the light.

If you think you know who I am
think twice, I'm convinced you understand
Look past the shadow and the stance----
the truth lies deeper than first glance.

No Disclaimer

At a time when whispers softly sway
and starlight drapes the edge of day
he walked alone, his stride was true
he was surely different from anyone she knew

He had a heart that danced to its own sweet tune
underneath the golden light of a Cajun moon
Confused and uncertain, no one could blame her
for he came with no warning, no fine print, no disclaimer

His laughter chased away the heavy gray
a breath of fresh air for a bright new day
Yet in her heart her worries did brew
a mysterious adventure uncharted and new

But still she lingered, drawn ever near
in the wake of his kindness, she felt no fear
With each fleeting moment, her spirit grew
embracing the peculiar man she finally knew

Caught

An inside voice forgot to whisper
secrets spill from a mental twister
doorways witness a private debate
thoughts argue aloud as they deliberate

Questions advocate, answers interrupt
hand gestures made to no one there
The room listens without judgement
chairs pretend not to stare

Caught mid-sentence, a verdict hanging in the air
no audience present to hear the notions she lay bare
Startled quiet, lips close on a thought, a grin fades
into a smile realizing she'd just been caught

The room keeps her secrets;
the clock keeps its tone
Sometimes, the truest conversations are
the one's when we're alone

Tin Can Dialogs I.

Are we not more than mere tin cans?
One said to the Other.
Dented by the weight of today's burdens,
the Other replied.

So here we sit, in this pantry of existence,
waiting for someone to hold us, and discover
our significance, expressed the First One.
Understanding that each, holds a universe of flavors,
all within reach, just waiting to be savored,
uttered the Last One.

Tin Can Dialogs II.

Are we not more than the labels placed upon us?
One asked the Other.
Forced to face the aisles of fate in a bargain contest,
the Other answered.

Why are the best sellers abused and tossed aside?"
the First One questioned.
Our contents spilled, our purpose misplaced,
a weakening in the protection we provide,
the Last One responded.

Tin Can Dialogs III.

I don't like the way, the rust clings to my edges,
one more layer, I'll be hanging over the ledges.
One said to the Other.

My rust is but the patina of my years, each ding
and dent, each tear, a souvenir, the Other responded.

It's the essence of life, the sum of our parts, portraying
individualism, like works of art, the First One stated.

It's a testament to time's slow erosion, aren't we vessels of
the Divine, even in this condition? the Last One inquired.

Tin Can Dialogs IV.

Remember the time when we were sealed tight.
We held the essence of life and did so with delight,
One said to the Other.

In our hearts we held the key, to the boundless depths of a journey's recipe, the Other replied.

Just echoing whispers of lives, we once knew, now discarded, flattened by a passing shoe, the First One remarked.

We still have the juice of ambition, the pulp of Love's cheer. Even in this condition, our life will persevere, the Last One stated.

Tin Can Dialogs V.

Now that time has changed our form,
and discolored our younger charm,
how many will it take to ease the pain?
How can we remember all the names?
One said to the Other.

Shameful, how when we're crumpled, damaged,
or drained, we're easily replaced with no reason
explained, the Other responded.

It's a new age now, one so different from before,
Our knowledge and experience don't matter anymore,
the First one expressed.

Is acceptance our best hope to survive?
I refused to believe the excuses they contrive,
the Last One stated.

Rage

The wind howls with a savage cry,
a tempest's rage, a hurricane's sigh.
Trees bow low, their branches frail and weak,
begging forgiveness, as nature's rage wreaks.

Waves crash hard against the shore,
a thunderous beast, an endless roar.
Battered rocks by fury unrestrained,
a dissonance of chords, chaos unchained.

The river's current, swift and strong,
a turbulent brute that knows no wrong.
Sweeping away all within its path,
a witness to nature's undaunting wrath.

Yet I'll stand firm upon my stone,
a quiet strength of my own.
I'll bend, I'll yield but will not break.
I'll rise again for my own life's sake.

Laughter

Laughter's love song, diverse yet true
a chorus of sounds, yellow, green, and blue
Giggles like tinkling bells, a silver chime
a whisper of amusement, a snippet in time

The chuckle, a gentle ripple in a stream
a secret shared, a whispered dream
The hoot, an owl's lively refrain
a witness to life's absurd and insane

The cackle, like a playful witches' spell
a mischievous melody, impossible to tell
The belly laugh, a rumbling from the deep
a hearty outburst, where laughter leaps

The roar, a thunderous burst of cheer
an earth-shaking revelry in full gear
The silent laugh, a shaking without sound
a secret glee, tightly wound

From tickling tales to witty jest
laughter finds refuge in every chest
No matter its shape, no matter its sound
in every laugh, a joy is found

The Eyes of Age

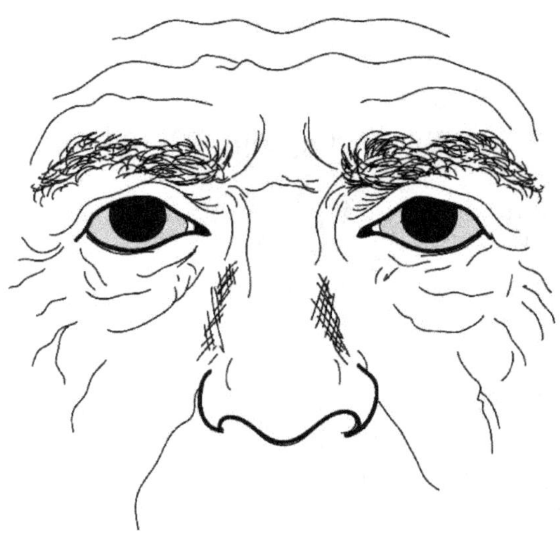

He walked where shadows cling
and felt the bite of Winter's sting
He's chased the sun, chased the rain
he's tasted loss and known the pain

He's learned that youth is swift to roam
yet only time can guide you home
The loudest voices rarely teach
only calm ones show what words can reach

He's seen dreams crumble, rise, then soar
and believes that less is often more
He's trodden with courage, paused with grace
let love and laughter mark his place

Wisdom is a secret garden
invisible to hurried eyes
Patience is the blossom
with a scent that satisfies

Seeing

Tell me. What is it you think you see
when you cast your eyes upon me?
Is it a curated smile, a practiced pose,
or is it something truer that shows?

Do you only see the polished public face,
the careful mask we learn to wear—
or can you sense the cracks beneath the
weight of stories hidden there?

Can you see the courage stitched into doubt?
The kindness given when no one's near,
the prayers whispered when my soul cries out,
the strength that conquers shadowed fear?

I am not the rumor, nor the outline others sketch.
I am the sum of quiet fights and truths
I haven't spoken yet, of whispered prayers
at midnight and dreams I won't forget.

I am the songs that linger
when the world has gone to sleep,
a story still unfolding
in a silence running deep.

Flocked

You may be a Douglas or Frasier Fir
yet no great outdoor fragrance occurs

You may be a massive white or blue Spruce
with no four-sided needles or cones to produce

You may be a Scotch or Virginia Pine
but never evergreen, hard to define

It's not time for Christmas, no holiday in view
yet with no reason why, some still flock you

Today

Today I walked a forgotten path, it's true,
seeking sights and experiences,
    the ones needing to be renewed.
    So, I silenced all the screens,
    turned off the digital allure,
    and listened closer than ever to nature's gentle
    cure.

Today I stretched out my hand to one I saw in need
    and watched how kindness bloomed, much like a
    nurtured seed.
I tilted my head back, and let the rain kiss my face,
    instead of running for cover, like others in the
    chase.

Today I sang my song aloud,
    though off-key it may seem,
and embraced the joy of living
    while fulfilling a dream.

Today I relearned to pause,
    to breathe, and simply be,
and embraced contentment
    in my own tranquility.

Truths

There's no blame that I'm trying to place,
it's just that some truths are double-faced.
Remembrance is a fickle friend,
each truth carries weight until the forgiving end.

My intensions stare back, taunting me,
with what ifs and maybes or both sides of the story.
Yet in the maze of thoughts and time,
lay treasured experiences of a lifetime.

So here I stand with an open embrace,
welcoming truths that put me in my place.

Emerge

Wake Up! You Live Here! Was that sound you heard far or near?
Did you notice the night or the day? Were there stars out?
Was the sky blue or gray? Did you notice the man you pass daily on the street?
Tell me, if you can, is it a smile or frown between his cheeks?

Wake Up! You Live Here! Did you share a hug today?
Or did you spend the day in fear? Isn't there a better way?
Did you say good morning to the lady with the cat?
Or did you turn your head, to avoid a friendly chat?

Wake Up! You Live Here! Do you know your neighbor's name?
Do you stop to say Hello, after all we're all the same.
Wake up! You Live Here! Do you feel the tender breeze?
Can you stop today and cheer and thank the Lord for the grass under the shade trees?

Generational Strangers

There're branches on the family tree unknown
untouched by greetings, visits postponed
Generational strangers, bound by grassroots' foothold
cousins far away, a lineage across the threshold

Children of children scattered across the country
too many schedules for a coordinated journey
Years have passed, lives drawn in parallel lines
untouched by greetings, communication flatlined

Then social media and a digital embrace
bridged the silent divide of time and space
Across the nation connections are found
three generations now on common ground

Misunderstood

He was a strange one, under the modern eye
a man who saw no point in the spinning of a lie.
Mostly perceived as a blunt, careless soul
words sharp and honest, often carrying a harsh toll

He spoke what he meant, though no malice
intended
just raw naked truth, nothing invented.
A barefoot riddle with no words to sugar-coat
a truth-teller's thorn, an ache in the footnote

Candor was his currency, laughter the receipt,
the echo of truth a wound bittersweet.
Regret is the shadow, forgiveness the plea—
a whispered surrender from who he used to be

Ghosted

She went to bed alone but not untouched.
The night evoked his name and
their memories clutched.

Nobody lay beside her
yet impressions pressed close.
In the absence where he stirred,
longing resided in his ghost.

Even the clock seemed to pause
listening to the quiet pulse of yearning.
The air held its breath, only because
cravings unmask a restless churning

Silent whispers drift through.
The night shadows dance within trembling light.
Memories go slow to soothe her passion,
each fleeting reverie sparks a quiet reaction.

Yet in the dawn, she'll rise and face the sun
another day begun, with the heartbeat of one.

In Sylvia's Room

Theres an untold story, now awakened,
a smoldering fire within, no longer forsaken.
In a quiet corner of her portion of the world,
a deep warmth spreads as her toes slowly curl.
An imprint of a man stirs her reflecting
heart, a tremor, a shiver, throughout every part.
His fingers strum the strings of her desire,
with replays of bliss in the heat of a wildfire.
Her breath falters, trembles, and purrs,
a rhythm of longing her body confers.
A satisfying pleasure at the thought of his
touch, a name unspoken but still means so much.

In Sylvia's room, there's an echo of a pulse
still unmet, a romance too fragile to last,
too intense to forget.

For the Love of Music

In a haze of spotlights, Elvis took the stage,
not for the fortune, nor to gauge
the roar of applause, the glitter, the gold—
but for the thrill that music alone can hold.

Each note he'd bend, gave a piece of his soul,
pouring himself out with tunes aimed to console.
Every wink, every chord, every sigh he shared,
revealed a man who deeply cared.

His voice strummed the heart strings of many,
a welcoming crowd brought him more than plenty.
Yet in the spotlight, humble and true,
he shared a magic, singing just for you.

When the stage had emptied, and lights dimmed low,
an echo remained long after the show.
No riches or applause could match the delight,
he got when he poured his heart out into the night.

For the love of music, and a thrill undefined
a sequenced silhouette would sparkle and shine.
With a quiver in his voice and a shiver of the knee,
the late Elvis Imposter sang you a personal melody

Listening

The wind spoke to me today.
A windowpane rattled
like it had something to say.
I leaned closer to the glass,
almost touching,
felt a cold rush of air
like fingers clutching.
A moment paused, then slipped past,
like something loved but not meant to last.
A quiet laugh, dialog from the edge of time,
a reminder that the ones who love us
is never left behind.

Morning Fog

I went out early,
before the world finished waking,
before the fog thought about vacating.
The ground was damp with yesterday's
thinking, a bird rehearsed a song
it would never be perfected but kept on singing.

I stood still long enough for my mind to
loosen its grip on the questions
that insist on answers, letting them slip.
Each thought returned not quite the same,
logic flickered like a dying flame.
I lingered still, caught in a silent stare,
knowing that reason drowns in stagnant air.

Ode to Cajun Country

I love the hush of a cypress dawn
where Spanish moss sways soft and low,
and bayous move like a sleepy yawn
through waters only pirogues know

I love the whistle of cane fields,
green rows bending in the heat
where sweat and sun were the shields
of calloused hand and aching feet

I love the way the elders speak,
French-laced words like weathered lace
voices gentle, proud, and unique
rooted deep in this mosquito infested place

I love the roll of an old accordion
crying out a Saturday night tune,
fiddles laughing in the union
of stars and a yellow Cajun moon

I love the dance on wooden floors,
boots that tap like summer rain,
two-steps spun through open doors
where joy outruns every pain

I love the porch lights flickering late
where truth and tall tales intertwine
in Cajun country hearts beat easy
and every story ages sweet like muscadines

I love the kitchens warm with spice—
roux stirred slow in a blackened pot,
gumbo thick as good advice,
and stories time has not forgot

I love this land that won't pretend—
where faith and family stand their ground,
and every stranger leaves a friend
in South Louisiana's Cajun towns.

Songbirds

I sang like a songbird today,
the ones with broken throats.
The off-key crow; the gull that gloats.
The rooster drunk on morning air,
the jay that screams but doesn't care.

My throat remembered what it once knew,
but the melody limped while rhythm flew.
I bruised the notes, crippled the refrain,
trying to sound like myself again.

Though my tune is obviously tattered and torn,
and my voice is certainly weathered and worn,
what rises then is a deeper art—
a sound made whole by a fearless heart.

I sang with the songbirds today,
we put our voices on display.
For the songs that live and never die,
    long after wings wave goodbye.

Sharp Objects

The keenest edge I've seen, silver-bright,
a sudden insertion, a sensuous lover's bite.
Betrayal of smiles slicing through the heart,
embracing the pain, lets the longing play its part.

I've felt the stiletto, a long slender threat,
an emotional piercing I can't forget.
Penetration of the heart, thin and deep,
the place where buried promises now sleep.

The carving blade, so finely honed,
with patient strokes my trust disowned.
Whittling the pieces of my thoughts,
to fit the blueprint one schemer sought.

Each sharp object, clean and true,
revealing the fragile self, I knew
My heart now bears the etched designs,
each mark a memory, carved line by line.

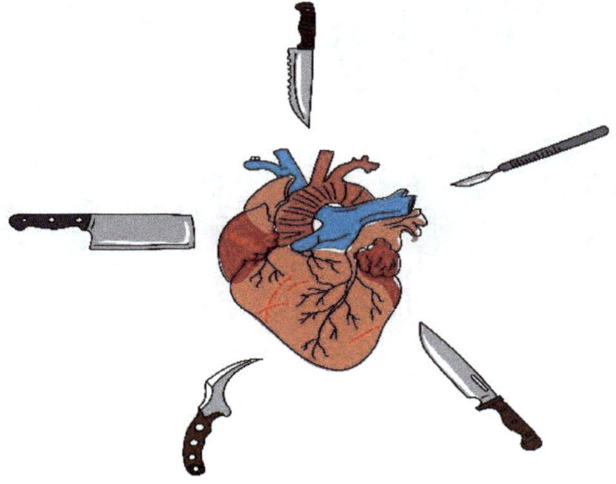

Isolation

I miss the ease of words that used to flow,
 no strain, no pause, no need to ask again— just know.
I miss the sound of voices soft and true,
 my loved one's call, a laugh I always knew.

Those tones, once clear, now drift beyond my reach,
 half-heard words in air, now common speech.
The small sounds fade— the birds, the rain, and music,
 now memories of my prime,
all those sounds that anchored me to my place
 and time.

 Words fall through cracks I cannot see,
  stories arrive, but their endings are missed by me.
 I learned to laugh a beat behind the room,
  to read a sentence only from a smile and presume.

The world grows distant, thinner, hard to claim,
 as silence slowly learns this speaker's name.
Confidence slips, a loss deep and dark,
 when conversations break, and responses miss their
 mark.

Winterthur

In the gardens of Winterthur, vibrant and bright,
more than flowers can bloom under leaf-filtered light.
In the not-so-distant past, a first meeting took place,
a location they agreed to meet, face to face.

Interesting conversations sitting on a park bench,
flavored with accents of New York and Cajun French.
Strolls along the garden's meandering paths,
among flowers and trees, between the giggles and laughs.

A picnic in a fairy garden, outside a stone cottage,
lit a light within them both at the highest wattage.
One kiss was given, and another one taken,
the magic of Winterthur had now overtaken.

As the seasons turn their pages one at a time,
perennials will bloom with your hand in mine.
Roots continue to deepen as we both grow,
love flourishes when tended, this we know.

Part three: Sidekicks

These poems play on the edges of thought and laughter—a mix of wit, wonder, and little truths that tag along for the ride.

Each one stands small but spirited.

They remind us that even the lightest lines can leave a lasting smile, or a scratch of the head.

Apparitions

Two apparitions floated into view,
could that one be me, and the other one you?
I believe it is, from what I see them do,
the memory of one, again to the rescue.

Who Are You?

"Who am I," You ask, with a twinkle and a smile.
A question I pondered, for quite a long while _____
"I haven't a clue," I uttered with a snicker and a sigh,
"Variations of a man, under a judging eye."

Unyielding Thorns

A clutched rose, fingers trembling and weak,
no sight to behold, no memories left to speak.
Love bleeds from hands, wrinkled and torn,
a network of scratches from unyielding thorns.

A Bitter Pill

Wisdom sensibly whispers,
        weakness silently answers
Both move like misfits,
        such awkward dancers
A natural fading,
        hastened by a war waged alone
A self-inflicted sentence
        turns a heart into stone
The truth is such a bitter pill—
        watching life erode
from a self-destructive will
        until pride lies aside its load.

Silence

Within the embrace of silence
when two hearts combine,
a brush of skin speaks volumes,
and words quietly decline.

A hush-bound dialog
privately fills the air,
with a silently sung song, and
seductive lingering stares.

With a breath held tight
inside the stillness of sound,
a quiet conversation takes place
when lips and tongues are tightly wound.

Louisiana Nights

Rain tapping on the window pane,
thunder's knocking at the door.
Another full moon night,
sleeping naked on the floor.

Humidity's steam bath,
drenched once again,
No change of clothes;
Don't touch me! shouts the skin.

Peculiar Old Man

Mama, tell me again, if you can,
that story about the peculiar old man.
You laughed so hard as you told it,
with such a radiant glow.
You said it was a memory molded,
from a pocketful of rainbows.

Heart To Heart

The fire crackles, casting shadows below,
across the worn-out rug there's a flickering glow.
They lay entwined, a tangled, sleepy heap,
their breath in sync, in a rhythm low and deep.

The night presents a canvas draped in stars,
their love a song, played on harps and guitars.
Her hand in his, a warm and steady prize,
two hearts speaking to each other without disguise.

The Journey Home

When the party's over
and I'm on my way home,
will I be heading north
or south?

Which will lose,
my heart or mouth?
When the party's over,
and I'm on my way home.

Doubles

Two haunting wolf moons, staring back at me
gravitational pull allows no eyes to see
Two invading suns on my horizon
geomagnetic storms, scrambling communication

Two wide rivers crisscrossing my path
reprimanding currents, a tormenting bath
Two north winds blowing furiously fast
one runs down my back, the other whistles
up my ass

Yes! It's True

Faith: a bright beacon illuminating our way,
Dispelling all shadows that attempt to sway.
His Love like a river flows with gentle might,
nurturing our souls with everlasting life

Wings

Fly beyond the edge of the sky
set your colors a blaze, don't ask why
Dance through storms, and laugh in the rain
turn doubts into wings and you'll fly again

Sing your story loud and true
paint the world with the light of you
Chase your dreams, bold and free
you're in charge of your own destiny

Unshaken

When the winds of doubt blow fierce and wild,
stand steadfast, like a trusting child.
When your hope seems lost and shadows reign,
faith whispers softly—rise again.
Through storms, through trials, you will endure,
all that is true will stand safe and secure.

Autumn

I'm no longer a fragile trembling shoot,
a sapling bent and damaged, withered and mute.
Leaves once verdant like two outstretched arms,
reflecting on seasons passed without qualm.

Blush

I see you now, my old friend and lover.
Visions dance, as my thoughts recover,
porcelain white skin, like sun-kissed snow,
shades of pink, a glistening blush in the afterglow.

There's a whisper of your name within the breeze,
a melodical wave of silence carrying memories.
A welcomed image, a phantom in the mind's
embrace,
fading shadows of two hearts misplaced.

The Answer Sleeps

Heaven hides its whisper well,
the question hangs like a weighted spell.
The answer sleeps, in the silent folds
where shadows sift.
Am I the next in line, the next to cross the rift?

Even the moons have no reply.
their truth moves on, and so do I.
Mind-wrought illusions, with and without sleep
of the three that remain, which will give
the final farewell speech?

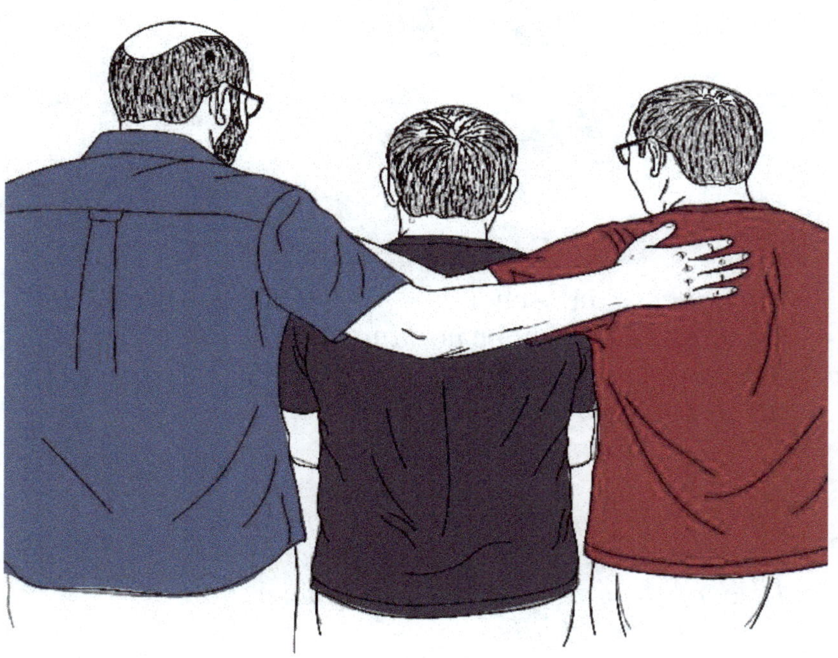

The Kitchen's Closed

I'm done! said the chef,
I've given it all, I have nothing left.
Far too often, nourishment falls short,
meals are now inventory,
I'm sorry to report.

Turn off the lights and lock the door,
the kitchen can offer nothing more.
Discard the apron, stained and worn thin,
there's a weight lifted
when you shed your old skin.

Verses

When the music has moved away
only the words come out to play
When the voice has faded and died
only the words have survived

It's the comfort of an old friend
when the page meets with ink, from my pen
I write in rhyme to see what they make
and let memories bloom for old times' sake

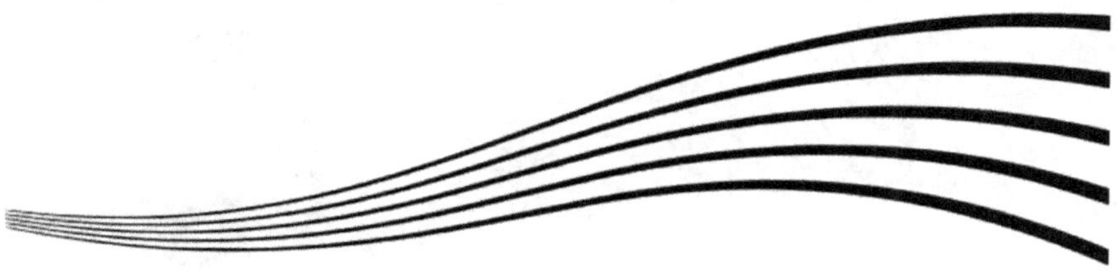

Happy are the Hearts (A Poem for Kara)

Happy are the hearts that look at you,
the joy of life shining through eyes of blue.

An angel's smile with dimples on her cheek,
the beauty of youth at its peak.

May your life be blessed like those you've touched,
and never forget, just how much
happy are the hearts that look at you.

A Fairy's Whisper

In lush fields where wildflowers dance,
Fairies Whisper secrets in a spiritual trance.
An unseen artist paints the sky with vibrant grace,
imagination holds us through life's uncertain chase.
Under the mushroom's dome, behind the veil of light,
dew drop baths after another silent flight.

Cajun Homesick

I miss the way the morning prayed in steam.
Coffee strong enough to wake a dream,
My mother humming hymns while the roux gets dark,
faith stirred slow before the day could start.

I miss the spice in the air, the fiddle's kick---
The accordion cries what my chest can't fix
No place holds me like that humid mix
of magnolias, bayous, and Sunday picnics

I miss the food, the faith, the way folks click
From porch-light laughter to crawfish thick
I miss the talk that needs no disguise,
truth told plain beneath Louisiana skies

No matter how far this old road bends,
I'll always find home where the bayou ends.
No cure exists, no easy fix----
There's only one thing to do when your Cajun
homesick

Limits

Limits live where some insist,
while others claim it doesn't exist.
They bend for some, for some it stays,
boundaries drawn in multiple ways.

Do they protect or merely bind?
Some swear it frees, some say confine.
They hide in rules, they hide in choice,
it speaks, yet some refuse to hear its voice.

Do they live within, or stand without?
Who draws the line, who casts the doubts?
Is it the measure of the world we see,
or a line that only seems to be.

Some break them boldly, some retreat,
others follow blindly; some repeat.
They shift with time, they shift with eyes,
they test the brave, mock the wise.

Is it a wall, a door, or sky?
A weight, a whisper, or a lie?
Do they guard, tempt, hide, or show.
It is, it isn't--- does anybody truly know?

Each person holds their own faint line,
a measure drawn by their own life's design.
Our limits wait, both near and far,
the quiet edge shaping who we are.

Devoured

Expectations come from near and far
tires rotating, spinning off the car
annotations fill the written page
footnotes of life arguing with age

Complications come from far and near
amplifications ring in my ears
illuminations fill an empty room
exposing all that darkness had consumed

Discord

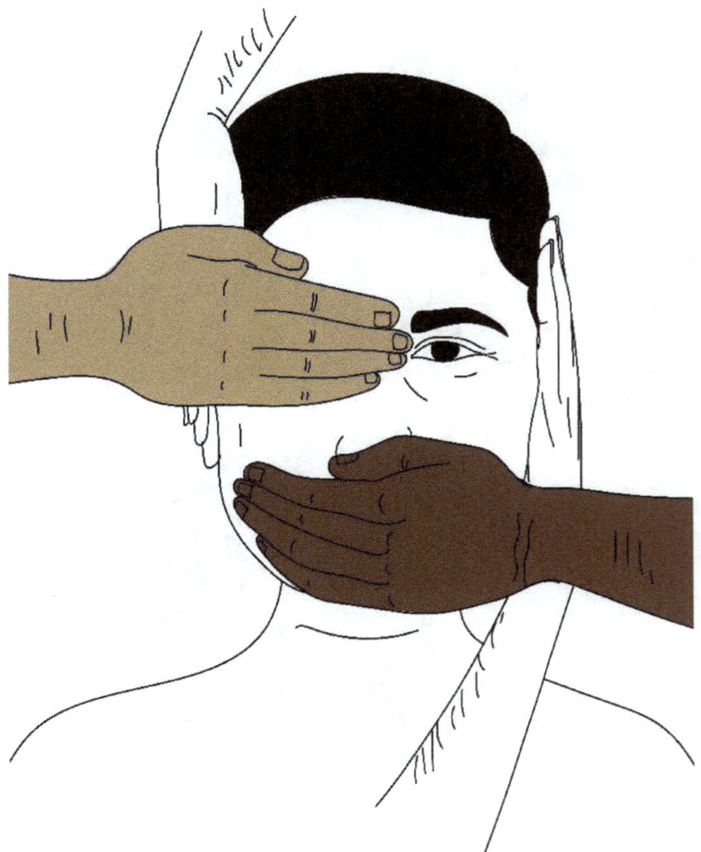

Deep within the drenched sound of Reason,
he listened and did not move.

Thought was there, a familiar beacon,
but still, Passion strongly disapproved.

He had trusted Reason many times before,
but this time Emotions made it unclear.

Thought argued hard, yet Passion wanted more,
and drowned the truth that brought him here.

Stoned

A stone sat above his head.
No name, no date, this is all it said:

Close your eyes old man,
        turn off the noise.
You've missed your ride,
        now accept your choice.
Broken promises and empty apologies,
        each will come to testify,
        like falling leaves in Autumn,
bones of reckoning pile high.

Venus and Mars

He's in and out, a quick escape,
a list, a plan, a steady pace.

She strolls the aisles, no rush, no race,
admiring things she'll never replace.

He puts things back where they belong,
she sets them down and moves along.

So different still, yet side by side,
in small mismatches, love resides.

Not meant to match in every way—
just meant to choose each other every day.

The Initiator

In the dance of an eight-legged ballet,
who was the spider, you say?
Who wove the web that magical day?
A silken mystery spun to never decay.

Was it curiosity that opened the door,
and allowed them in to play?
Each insisting the other wove strands
to catch their prized prey.
A braided veil with such delicate grace,
one that time itself could only embrace.

Fear

A tremor in his being, a constant hum
Afraid he was, fear was his drum
He built a world where he could hide away
and in that place, he slowly went astray

His memories like phantoms danced and swayed
In and out of sight, what a strange bed he made
He chased the light but stumbled in the dark
A flickering flame until his last dying spark

Stillness within Green Glass

Air rearranges itself whenever she enters
not as movement but as consent
As if something older than breath
has recognized her and stepped aside

Stillness leans toward her
as if gravity has learned a new prayer
Nothing moves but everything shifts
as fate does whenever it's there

Bathing with Nature

Filtered light dispersed
on the forest floor
highlights on a pine
stripped of its flaky bark

A work of art not there
moments before
tattoos of nature
revealing its mark

In dappled light where
silent breezes dance
a canopy of leaves sway
in a gentle trance

A pine tree stands, its bark stripped bare
Revealing nature's canvas smooth and fair

Like tattoos etched upon a living scroll
a woodpecker's drill-like beak pierced its soul

About the Author

Darryl Broussard, known by friends as Deke, is a singer songwriter turned poet whose voice was born on the banks of the Bayou Teche in New Iberia, Louisiana. From an early age, music shaped his way of seeing the world.

What began as a boy's fascination with melody and lyrics, evolved into a lifelong devotion to the art of expression. Weaving thoughts and melody, his poetry carries a natural beat and rhythm in words and meaning.

His work delivers the warmth of his Cajun roots and the grit of a man unafraid to speak his truth. Bold, intense, and a little peculiar, he approaches every poem with the same passion he once poured into his songs—seeking to connect, to stir, and to remind us that beauty often hides in life's smallest, most unexpected places.

Through his writing, Deke continues to blend the lyricism of his musical background with the quiet reckoning of poetry, creating works that provoke a smile, a thought, a memory, a question, or the unexpected.

Reader Beware!

A voice truly shaped by resilience, hope, and the spirit within us all.

So happy you've met Deke.

www.ingramcontent.com/pod-product-compliance
Lightning Source LLC
LaVergne TN
LVHW010614110826
845149LV00003B/905

* 9 7 9 8 9 9 0 4 5 3 6 7 8 *